Danger

by
David Orme

Thunderbolts

Danger
by David Orme

Illustrated by Katie Wood

Published by Ransom Publishing Ltd.
Radley House, 8 St. Cross Road, Winchester, Hants. SO23 9HX, UK
www.ransom.co.uk

ISBN   978 178127 062 2

First published in 2013

Copyright © 2013 Ransom Publishing Ltd.

Illustrations copyright © 2013 Katie Wood
'Get the Facts' section - images copyright: cover, prelims, passim – Daniel Brunner, Chris McNaught; pp 4/5 - imagedepotpro; pp 6/7 - Kontizas Dimitrios; pp 8/9 - Pavel Ševela, Morio, Burtonpe; pp 10/11 - eriktham, Jelson25, t_kimura; pp 12/13 - Robert Pears, Wicki58, Terry J Alcorn, svengine; pp 14/15 - Chris Dascher, Alvesgaspar, Mithril, koles; pp 16/17 - Stannered, UK Crown copyright, Roulex_45, Woodennature, Simone Becchetti; pp 18/19 - Brocken Inaglory, Scientif38, David Rydevik, Steven W. Dengler; pp 20/21 - Hexogen, Denis Janssen; pp 22/23 - michele Galli, Daniel R. Burch, helissente; p 36 - Chris Rogers.

A CIP catalogue record of this book is available from the British Library.

All rights reserved. No part of this publication may be reproduced, stored in a retrieval system, or transmitted, in any form or by any means, electronic, mechanical, photocopying, recording or otherwise, without the prior permission of the publishers.

The rights of David Orme to be identified as the author and of Katie Wood to be identified as the illustrator of this Work have been asserted by them in accordance with sections 77 and 78 of the Copyright, Design and Patents Act 1988.

page 5

page 25

Danger: The Facts

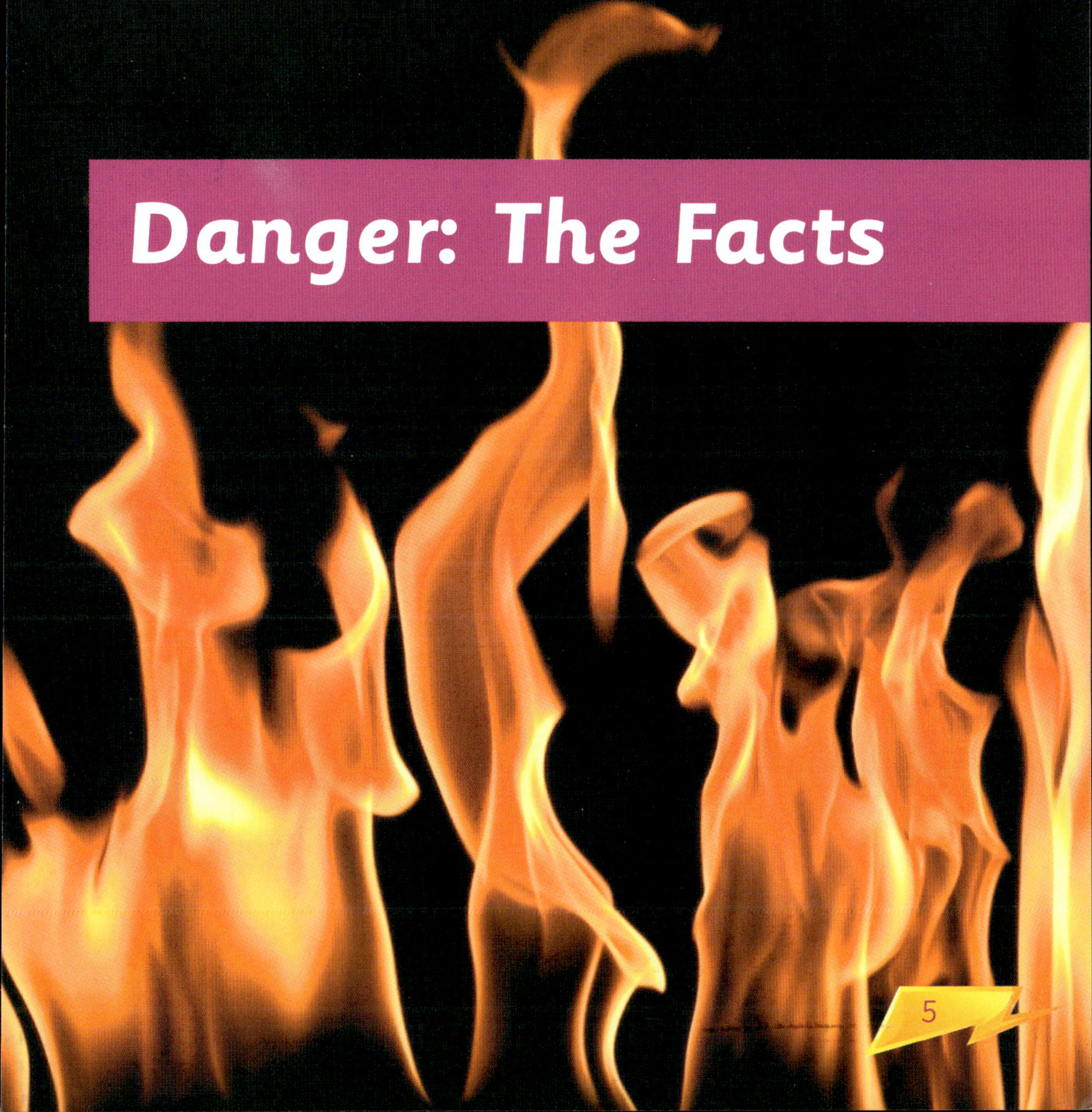

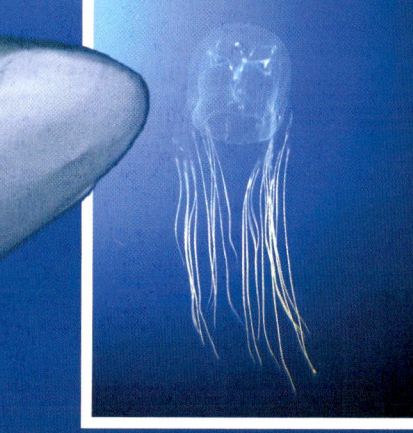